# Fighting Back

David Downing

**WORLD ALMANAC® LIBRARY**

Please visit our web site at: www.worldalmanaclibrary.com
For a free color catalog describing World Almanac® Library's list of
high-quality books and multimedia programs, call 1-800-848-2928 (USA)
or 1-800-387-3178 (Canada). World Almanac® Library's fax: (414) 332-3567.

Library of Congress Cataloging-in-Publication Data

Downing, David, 1946-
    Fighting back / by David Downing.
        p. cm. — (World Almanac Library of the Holocaust)
    Includes bibliographical references and index.
    ISBN 0-8368-5946-4 (lib. bdg.)
    ISBN 0-8368-5953-7 (softcover)
    1. World War, 1939-1945—Jewish resistance—Juvenile literature.  2. Holocaust,
Jewish (1939-1945)—Juvenile literature.  I. Title.  II. Series.
    D810.J4D694  2005
    940.53'1832—dc22                                                    2005040775

First published in 2006 by
**World Almanac® Library**
A Member of the WRC Media Family of Companies
330 West Olive Street, Suite 100
Milwaukee, WI  53212  USA

Copyright © 2006 by World Almanac® Library.

Produced by Discovery Books
Editors: Geoff Barker, Sabrina Crewe, and Jacqueline Gorman
Designer and page production: Sabine Beaupré
Photo researchers: Geoff Barker and Rachel Tisdale
Map: Stefan Chabluk
Consultant: Ronald M. Smelser, Professor of Modern German History, University of Utah
World Almanac® Library editorial direction: Mark J. Sachner
World Almanac® Library editor: Alan Wachtel
World Almanac® Library art direction: Tammy West
World Almanac® Library production: Jessica Morris

Photo credits: cover: USHMM, courtesy of Samuel Gruber; title page: Topfoto.co.uk; p. 4: Hanan
Isachar/Corbis; p 7: Topfoto.co.uk; p. 9: USHMM, courtesy of Dr. Rudolf Jacobson; p. 10: Anne Frank
House, Amsterdam/Getty Images; p. 11: USHMM, courtesy of Peter Feigel; p. 12: USHMM, courtesy of
Raphael Scharf; p. 14: USHMM, courtesy of Zydowski Instytut Historyczny, Instytut Naukowo-Badawczy;
p. 17: Mary Evans Picture Library/Weimar Archive; p. 18: Topfoto.co.uk; p. 19: Keystone/Getty Images;
p. 20: USHMM, courtesy of Donald Schaufelberger; p. 22: Michael St. Maur/Corbis; p. 23: USHMM,
courtesy of Belarussian State Archive of Documentary Film and Photography; p. 24: Topfoto.co.uk; p. 28:
USHMM, courtesy of Moshe Kaganovich; p. 31: USHMM, courtesy of Vitka Kampner Kovner; p. 33: Mary
Evans Picture Library; p. 34: Topfoto.co.uk; p. 36: USHMM, courtesy of Barbara Roth; p. 38: USHMM,
courtesy of Avi Granot; p. 40 (left): Corbis; p. 40 (right): USHMM; p. 43: USHMM, courtesy of Instytut
Pamieci Narodowej.

Printed in Canada

1 2 3 4 5 6 7 8 9 09 08 07 06 05

*Cover:* These Jewish resistance fighters, led by partisan Yehiel Grynszpan, operated in the Parczew
Forest in Poland. Many partisan groups formed to fight against Nazi persecution.

*Title page:* Jews in Warsaw, Poland, rose up in rebellion against the Nazis during the Warsaw Ghetto
uprising of 1943.

# Contents

# The Holocaust

## The Murder of Millions

The word *holocaust* has a long history. In early times, it meant a burnt offering to the gods, and in the **Middle Ages**, a huge sacrifice or destruction. It still has this second meaning today, particularly when used to describe large-scale destruction by fire or nuclear weapons. But since the 1970s, the word has gained a new and specific meaning. Today, when people refer to the Holocaust—with a capital "H"—they mean the murder of approximately six million Jews by Nazi Germany and its **allies** during World War II.

This crime had deep historical roots. In predominantly Christian Europe, the Jews had always been considered a race apart and had often endured persecution for that reason. When governments or peoples wanted someone to blame for misfortune, they often picked on an innocent, and helpless Jewish minority.

In the early twentieth century, many Germans wanted someone to blame for their defeat in World War I and the terrible economic hardship that

**This sculpture at the Yad Vashem Holocaust Memorial in Jerusalem, Israel, symbolizes the deportation of the Jews to the death camps.**

followed. They, too, picked on the Jews in their midst—with ultimately horrific results. The Holocaust was ordered and organized by political leaders, carried out by thousands of their willing supporters, and allowed to happen by millions of ordinary people.

The scale of the crime is still hard to take in. To use a modern comparison, about three thousand people were killed in the **terrorist** attacks in the United States on September 11, 2001. Between June 1941 and March 1945, an average of four thousand European Jews were murdered every day.

These people were killed in a variety of ways. Some were left to starve, some to freeze. Many were worked to death in **labor camps**. More than one million were shot and buried in mass graves. Several million were gassed to death in specially built **extermination camps** such as Auschwitz and Treblinka.

## The Persecution of the Jews

The Jews were not the only victims of the Nazis. In fact, it is probable that the Nazis and their allies murdered at least five million other **civilians** before and during World War II. Their victims were killed for a variety of reasons: **communists** for their political opinions, **homosexuals** for their sexual orientation, people with mental disabilities for their supposed uselessness to society, **Gypsies** and Slavs for their supposed racial inferiority, and Russians, Poles, and other eastern Europeans because they happened to be in the Nazis' way.

The central crime in the Holocaust—the murder of millions of Jews—was a long time in the making. Most of the actual killing took place between 1941 and 1945, but the Jews of Germany were subject to intense persecution from the moment Adolf Hitler and his Nazi Party took power in 1933. That persecution was itself merely the latest in a series of persecutions stretching back over almost two thousand years, in which every nation of Europe had at some time played a part.

This book looks at the many ways in which Jews fought back against the Holocaust and at the help they received from governments and individuals both inside and outside Europe.

# CHAPTER ONE

# The Difficulties of Fighting Back

## Like Lambs to the Slaughter?

After World War II ended, some people—Jews and non-Jews alike—wondered out loud why the Jews had allowed themselves to be systematically murdered in such huge numbers. Surely, they suggested, the Jews could have resisted more.

Such opinions were based in ignorance. For one thing, these opinions did not take into account the enormous difficulties involved in organizing and sustaining **resistance**. For another, they ignored how much resistance the Jews had actually put up.

## An Uneven Contest

Resistance was difficult for a number of reasons. The Nazis could use overwhelming force against any Jewish community in occupied Europe. The **ghettos**, labor camps, **concentration camps**, and **death camps** were surrounded by high fences and guarded by heavily armed men. Any form of defiance or protest was punished with breathtaking severity, and that punishment was often applied to the whole community, not just to the protesters. Since individual acts of resistance were likely to result in the punishment of the whole community, any Jew who resisted was also risking the lives of his or her family, friends, and neighbors. In the unlikely event of a serious rebellion, the local Nazi commandant could always call in reinforcements.

The Jews rarely had any weapons at their disposal, and any weapons they might have had were no match for their enemy's. Moreover, most Jews in the ghettos and camps were seriously weakened by hunger, ill health, and ill treatment, and the separate communities had little contact with each other, so it was hard to

**Barbed wire still surrounds the infamous Auschwitz camp—now the Auschwitz Museum—where more than a million Jews were put to death.**

coordinate efforts. Throughout the years of the Holocaust, the Jews of Europe received little help from others. In fact, there were few people they could turn to for help.

And yet, despite these enormous difficulties, many Jews did resist. In the ghettos, the camps, and the forests, they fought against the Nazis. Thousands of men, women, and children tried to evade capture and to escape if they were caught. With heads and hearts and hands, they fought for their dignity and their lives.

## Resistance in Czestochowa

In January 1943, several members of the secret Jewish Fighting Organization in the Polish city of Czestochowa were accidentally caught in an **SS** round-up of Jews for deportation. Only one man, Mendel Fiszlewicz, had a gun, and he decided that resistance was the only hope. He managed to shoot the SS officer in charge, but then his gun jammed, and he was quickly killed by the other SS men.

The SS shot twenty-five other men as an immediate reprisal and sent an extra three hundred women and children from Czestochowa to the **gas chambers** in Treblinka. The intended lesson was clear— in the event of resistance, not only the resisters would be killed but also huge numbers of their fellow Jews.

# CHAPTER TWO

# Refusing to Be Caught

## No Escape

Before World War II began, many Jews left Germany for western European countries such as France and the Netherlands. When Germany invaded Poland in 1939, many Polish Jews managed to escape eastward into the Soviet Union. By the end of 1941, however, military conquests—and Germany's invasion of the Soviet Union—had brought most of these Jews back under German control. In addition, the virtual sealing of Europe's borders had made further **emigration** almost impossible. Before war broke out, a few thousand Jews had managed to reach the safety of Morocco, Palestine, or the Far East, but most were now trapped. Unable to escape, those who wished to avoid imprisonment in ghettos or camps had to go into hiding.

## Living as "Submarines"

Where could they hide? For many Jews, the answer was simple: in plain sight. They posed as non-Jews, living what looked (from the outside) like normal lives. In reality, they lived in a state of almost nonstop anxiety. There was always the chance that someone would notice that their **identity papers** were forged, or that someone would recognize them and inform the Nazis, or that they would make a mistake and give themselves away.

Many did succeed in staying hidden. Edith Hahn, a young Jewish woman from Vienna, Austria, moved to Munich, Germany, with a non-Jewish friend's identity papers. (The friend told the authorities that she had lost them.) Hahn started a new life as a non-Jew. A Nazi officer fell in love with her, married her, and protected her after she told him she was Jewish. In Berlin, Germany's capital, as many as five thousand Jews survived to the end of the war by hiding or by posing as non-Jews. Many received help from non-Jews, but some had

An identity card issued by the **Third Reich**. The large red letter "J" (for *Jude*), which is stamped across the details on the left, showed that the bearer, Margarete Sara Jacobsohn, was Jewish.

## One Life against Thirty

"Professor Bergman, a fragile and kindly man, was rocking his infant son, trying to stop his coughing. On the other side of the trapdoor above us came shouts of German search parties and the barking of their dogs.

"We all fell silent; only the baby's coughing continued. 'Shhh,' hissed a burly man near the door. The coughing did not stop. The man crawled over and placed a hand on the baby's mouth. The coughing ceased. Minutes passed. The child sank limply to the ground.

"All the while, Professor Bergman sat petrified. I knew he was not a coward. Even then, I understood that if he could think or feel anything at all, he was weighing one life against thirty, even if that life was his own son's."

*Samuel Pisar, describing an event that happened while he and his mother were hiding in an underground bunker during a period when Jews were being **deported** from the Bialystok Ghetto in Poland*

**This movable bookcase in the house where the Franks hid in Amsterdam concealed secret rooms. Anne Frank and her family hid in these rooms for more than two years.**

only their own wits and courage to protect them.

In Poland and the western Soviet Union, many Jews sought safety in the large forests that dotted the area. Some died from hunger and cold, but others survived to join the **partisan** groups that operated in these forests.

## Hidden by Gentiles

Most of Europe's Jews-in-hiding were hidden by **gentiles**. All across the continent, in both cities and the countryside, gentile families sheltered individual Jews and sometimes whole Jewish families. Sometimes they sheltered them openly, claiming that the Jews were part of their own families; sometimes Jews were carefully hidden away from the prying eyes of neighbors.

The punishment for hiding Jews was usually execution, and many non-Jews engaged in this highly dangerous activity for only one reason: money. The Nazi authorities knew this and offered to pay even more money if Jews were turned in. Many non-Jews did hand over the people they were hiding to the Nazis. Many more Jews were not turned in, but some were treated as little better than slaves by those they had paid to keep their families hidden from the Nazis.

Other gentiles took the same risks out of kindness or love. In Amsterdam, in the Netherlands, Anne Frank and her family were hidden and fed for two years by her father's gentile business partners, beginning in July 1942. They remained in their hiding place until they were betrayed to the Nazis in August 1944. Other hidden Jews were more fortunate, remaining undetected until the Nazis were driven from their towns or areas.

**Les Grillons guest house was one of many places in the French village of Le Chambon-sur-Lignon that gave sanctuary to Jewish children during the war.**

The people of Le Chambon-sur-Lignon, a small town in southeastern France close to the Swiss border, chose to help Jews on the run because they believed it was the right thing to do. By the end of war, several thousand Jewish adults and children had been taken in by individual families, placed in group homes, or smuggled across the border into Switzerland.

## Hiding in the Country

"I was sent to this farm, to live with people I did not know. . . . There were three girls in the family. I can't say that I suffered, but I was lonely. I had no friends. They were good to me, but sometimes, the youngest, who was fourteen, would say things to me like, 'You dirty Jew.' . . .

"One day I saw soldiers with rifles coming to the farm. The farmer's wife put me in the bedroom, under the mattress. I got out and went to look through the keyhole and I could see the Nazis in the next room. I was lucky. They didn't search the place."

*Rosette Goldstein, who was born in 1938 and spent several years hiding on a gentile family's farm in France*

# Resistance in the Ghettos

## Survival Comes First

Between the start of World War II in September 1939 and the Nazi decision to murder all of Europe's Jews in the fall of 1941, official Nazi policy toward the Jews was to force them into separate areas of towns and cities called ghettos. During this period, the main priority for Jewish inhabitants of the ghettos was, at first, simply to survive. There was never enough food, water, or heating in the ghettos, and two or more families frequently

**An emaciated Jewish boy sits on a sidewalk in the Warsaw Ghetto in Poland, where almost half a million people lived under the Nazis. This was one of many pictures taken by German soldier Willy Georg in 1941.**

had to share a single room. Diseases spread quickly, and medicines were hard to come by. People did what they could to provide for themselves and their families. They sold what they had, opened businesses inside the ghetto, grew vegetables in the tiny areas of dirt that were available, and smuggled in what they could from outside.

This struggle to survive involved some cooperation with the Nazis, who set up a Jewish council, or **Judenrat**, in each ghetto. In exchange for sending their fittest people to work in Nazi factories and labor camps, the *Judenräte* were allowed to police the ghettos themselves and decide who got what share of the few resources available.

## Secret Resistance

There was little open resistance to the Nazis in the early years of the ghettos. Rather than take the dangerous step of confronting their persecutors, most Jewish leaders decided on a form of secret resistance—they would keep their culture alive within the ghetto walls. All the ghetto councils organized secret schools and classes for children. And even though the Nazis attempted to suppress religion and culture, ghetto residents held services and put on plays and concerts. Ghetto leaders encouraged community life to continue as much as possible.

### The Partisan's Anthem

*Hirsh Glik was inspired to write his "Jewish Partisan's Anthem" by the heroic failure of the Warsaw Ghetto uprising. The song was carried across occupied Europe by word-of-mouth and became an anthem for all Jewish partisan groups. This is the first and last verse:*

"Never say that you have reached the final road
Though lead-grey clouds conceal blue skies above
The hour that we have longed for now draws near
Our steps proclaim like drumbeats: We are here!"

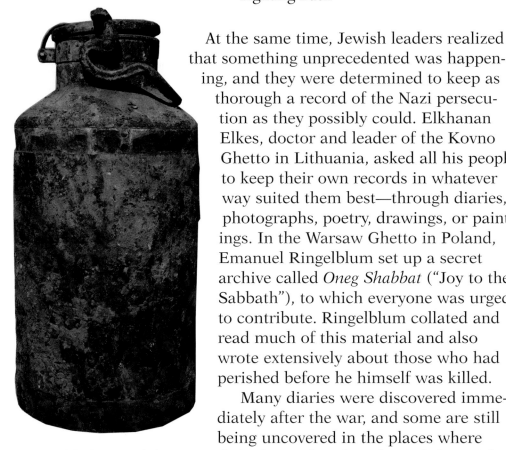

At the same time, Jewish leaders realized that something unprecedented was happening, and they were determined to keep as thorough a record of the Nazi persecution as they possibly could. Elkhanan Elkes, doctor and leader of the Kovno Ghetto in Lithuania, asked all his people to keep their own records in whatever way suited them best—through diaries, photographs, poetry, drawings, or paintings. In the Warsaw Ghetto in Poland, Emanuel Ringelblum set up a secret archive called *Oneg Shabbat* ("Joy to the Sabbath"), to which everyone was urged to contribute. Ringelblum collated and read much of this material and also wrote extensively about those who had perished before he himself was killed.

**This is one of the two milk cans in which Emanuel Ringelblum hid and buried his secret archives of life in the Warsaw Ghetto.**

Many diaries were discovered immediately after the war, and some are still being uncovered in the places where their doomed authors buried them. They provide us with a vivid picture of what life in the ghettos was like: the terrible hardships and sudden moments of joy, the petty annoyances and the mind-numbing terror. Those who wrote these diaries were refusing to die in silence.

Paintings and drawings were also hidden away, and many of these were later found. Artist Esther Lurie created more than four hundred watercolors and drawings during her four years in the Kovno Ghetto. Another artist, Josef Schlesinger, produced a painting of a public execution in the same ghetto. Many poems and songs, some written down at the time and other remembered and recorded later, have survived from the ghettos. Some of the works were angry, some were sad, and some—like many of the lullabies created in the ghettos—were heartbreaking.

## A Ghetto Diary

"Wednesday, 22 July 1942: A day of turmoil, chaos and fear: the news about the deportation of Jews is spreading like lightning through the town. Jewish Warsaw has suddenly died, the shops are closed. Jews run by, in confusion, terrified. The Jewish streets are an appalling sight—the gloom is indescribable. There are dead bodies in several places. . . . Beggar children are being rounded up into wagons.

"Friday, 31 July 1942: The tenth day of the slaughter that has no parallel in our history. . . . They are driving the old people from the old people's home at 52 Nowolopki Street. Those rounded up are divided up into those fit for work, those able to survive and those not fit to be transported. The last group is killed on the spot.

"Wednesday, 5 August 1942: The 'action' continues unabated. We have no more strength to suffer. There are many murders. They kill the sick who don't go down to the courtyards."

*From the Warsaw Ghetto diary of Abraham Levin, which formed part of Emanuel Ringelblum's secret archive of the ghetto. Levin was killed by the Germans in January 1943.*

## Bravery in the Face of Death

By mid-1942, it had become clear to most ghetto leaders that they and their people were all going to be killed, whether or not they cooperated with the Nazis. Some people in the ghettos had always argued for either open **noncooperation** or violent resistance, and now their numbers grew dramatically. If they were going to be killed anyway, what did they have to lose?

Noncooperation could take many forms, and most of them—as their participants already knew—were likely to be fatal. Anyone refusing an order from a German was usually shot on the spot. Adam Czerniakow, leader of the Warsaw *Judenrat*, knew what would happen to him if he refused the order to assemble six thousand of his people each day for deportation, but he still couldn't do it. He killed himself instead. By doing this, Czerniakow resisted the Nazis in the only way he

## A Ghetto Lullaby

"God has closed down the world,
And all around us is night
It awaits us with shuddering
    and fear
We both stand here,
In this hard, hard hour,
And the path leads who knows
    where.

We were chased from home
Stripped to the bone,
Through the dark, driven into
    the field,
And hail, snow and wind
Accompanied you, my child,
Accompanied you into the abyss
    of the world."

*Lullaby written by Yeshayahu
Szpigel in the Lodz Ghetto*

could, by sticking to his principles and then taking his own life before the Nazis could kill him.

Janusz Korczak, a doctor and teacher, ran an orphanage in the Warsaw Ghetto. A respected professor, he received many offers of help to escape from the ghetto, but he refused to leave his children. When told to prepare the two hundred children for deportation, Korczak led them to the station, looked after them on the train, and died with them in the Treblinka death camp. Looking after the children to the bitter end was Korczak's way of resisting the inhuman acts of the Nazis.

## Open Resistance

Other Jews increasingly favored open resistance, regardless of the consequences to themselves or their communities. When the United Partisan Group, a resistance group from the Vilna Ghetto in Lithuania, wrecked several military trains, the Nazis threatened to burn the whole ghetto down if the group's leader, Yitzhak Wittenberg, was not handed over to them. The *Judenrat* gave in, deciding they had to put the interests of the community above that of one individual. When Wittenberg escaped, worse threats followed, and he gave himself up. He committed suicide in prison by taking poison.

As it became increasingly obvious that all Jews were under the sentence of death, such threats lost their force, and open resistance became more common. In December 1942, Jewish resisters in the Krakow Ghetto in Poland attacked and killed several SS officers in a café. These resisters realized that their attack would make little or no difference to the outcome of the war. They expected to be hunted down and killed in a few days, and most of them were. What mattered to them, as one wrote later, was "to save what could be saved—at least honor."

Many **revolts** occurred at the point of deportation, when young Jews decided to die fighting rather than meekly board the trains to the death camps. When the three thousand Jews of the Tuczyn Ghetto in southeastern Poland were ordered to assemble for deportation, they started burning anything that might be useful to the Nazis. As local troops tried to stop them, the fires raged out of control. In the confusion, some two thousand Jews escaped into the surrounding forests. Most were recaptured, but a few survived.

## The Warsaw Ghetto Uprising

The most famous act of ghetto resistance was the Warsaw Ghetto uprising of April and May 1943. It was the first and largest general urban uprising against the Germans in occupied Europe. The Warsaw Ghetto, once so large, contained many fewer Jews by 1943. Deportations to Treblinka (which began in July 1942) and terrible conditions had reduced the ghetto's

**In May 1943, survivors of the Warsaw Ghetto uprising are rounded up for deportation by German soldiers.**

**Jewish fighters are pictured with one of their few machine guns during the Warsaw Ghetto uprising.**

population from almost 0.5 million to less than 70,000. Knowing that they would all be deported, the survivors decided to resist. In 1942, they formed the Jewish Fighting Organization, which had the slogan, "Brothers, don't die in silence. Let's fight!" They began to smuggle weapons into the ghetto.

In January 1943, SS troops were fired on when they entered the ghetto to round up more Jews for deportation. Over the next few days, thousands of Jews were taken prisoner, but twenty-two SS troops were killed and more than fifty were wounded. The Germans, who had been planning a third action, then withdrew from the ghetto. For two months, they left it alone. The Jews were convinced their resistance had deterred the Nazis and began plans for future armed struggle. During those months, the Jewish Fighting Organization smuggled in more weapons and ammunition and built a maze of underground tunnels. When the Germans returned on April 19 with the intention of deporting all the remaining inhabitants of the ghetto, they found themselves in a real fight.

The Jews had far fewer and far less effective weapons than the Nazis, but they managed to hold out for almost one month. As the end drew near in the middle of May, a few Jews escaped

## A Call to Resist

"Do not go willingly to death! Fight for life to the last breath. Greet our murderers with teeth and claws, with axe and knife, with hydrochloric acid and iron crowbars. Make the enemy pay for blood with blood, for death with death!

"Will you hide in mouse-holes when they drag out your dear ones to dishonor and death?!

"Let us fall upon the enemy in time, kill and disarm him. Let us stand up against the criminals and if necessary die like heroes. If we die in this way we are not lost!

"Make the enemy pay dearly for your lives! Take revenge for the Jewish centers that have been destroyed and for the Jewish lives that have been extinguished."

*Appeal by the Jewish Self-Defense Organization
in the Bialystok Ghetto in Poland*

into the rest of the city, where some, with help from non-Jews, survived in hiding for the remainder of the war. Seven thousand ghetto residents were killed in the fighting, and another thirty thousand were immediately shipped off to Treblinka. Those buildings that remained were flattened to the ground.

**Jewish resistance fighters are led away during the Warsaw Ghetto uprising in spring 1943. The original German caption to this photo was "bandits."**

# CHAPTER FOUR

# Resistance in the Camps

## Under Constant Watch

If resistance was hard to organize and maintain in the ghettos, it was even harder in the camps. Some camps were certainly harsher and more secure than others, but the levels of supervision and security in all of them were much closer and tighter than in the ghettos. The camps were surrounded by high wire fences, overlooked by watchtowers, and constantly patrolled by guards.

Prisoners—and particularly Jewish prisoners—were kept weak by lack of food and ill-treatment. They were allowed very little private space or time. In some cases, they could communicate with each other only while locked in their barracks during the hours of darkness, and then only in

**Prisoners at Mauthausen exchange news through the fence separating the "sick" and "working" sections of the concentration camp. Mauthausen was infamous, even among concentration camps, for the brutal treatment of its inmates.**

whispers under their threadbare blankets. Informers were everywhere, so talking to strangers was always dangerous. In such circumstances, organizing even small acts of resistance was full of danger.

As in the ghettos, the needs of simple survival came first. Because disobedience invited execution or other consequences (such as transfer to a punishment unit, which amounted to much the same thing as execution), prisoners kept their heads down and tried to follow orders as quickly and efficiently as they could. They avoided eye contact with the guards and tried to stay on the right side of the **Kapos**, who usually decided each person's share of the available food.

## Leaving Word Behind

In the camps, as in the ghettos, there was an attempt to keep Jewish culture—and hope—alive. Where it was possible, religious services were held in secret. When they could, Jewish inmates kept diaries. Salmen Gradowski, a member of the

## Hanukkah in a Labor Camp

"It was the cold winter of 1944 and although we had nothing like calendars, my father, who was my fellow prisoner there, took me and some of our friends to a corner in our barrack. He announced that it was the eve of **Hanukkah**, produced a curious-shaped clay bowl, and began to light a wick immersed in his precious, but now melted, margarine ration. Before he could recite the blessing, I protested at this waste of food. He looked at me—then at the lamp—and finally said: 'You and I have seen that it is possible to live up to three weeks without food. We once lived almost three days without water. But you cannot live properly for three minutes without hope.' "

*Hugo Gryn remembering Hanukkah in Lieberose labor camp*
*(a subcamp of Sachsenhausen) when he was fourteen years old*

Auschwitz **Sonderkommando** who witnessed the murder of his family and was himself eventually gassed, was one of many who buried messages in the ashes of the victims. "Dear finder," his letter began, "search everywhere, in every inch of soil. Tens of documents are buried under it, mine and those of other persons, which will throw light on everything that was happening here."

## Mala and Edward

In Auschwitz, Mala Zimetbaum, a Belgian Jew, became an interpreter—she spoke several languages—and a messenger, carrying messages across the huge camp complex. She became both well-known and popular. When she and her boyfriend, a young Polish Jew named Edward Galinski, managed to escape from the camp in stolen SS uniforms in June 1944, there was rejoicing among other prisoners. Mala and Edward were recaptured a couple of weeks later. Back in camp, both were tortured. They both attempted (but failed) to take their own lives before they could be killed, Edward by hanging himself, Mala by slitting her wrists. The whole camp was saddened by their deaths, but many also celebrated their two weeks at liberty as a victory over the Nazis.

In Auschwitz, the walls and ceilings of some barracks were covered with paintings that can still be seen today. Some prisoners, such as Polish painter and former *Sonderkommando* David Olère, held the horrors he had seen in his memory until after the war. He was finally able to draw and paint the scenes after he was released.

## Sabotage

Those who worked as slaves in the factories, quarries, and mines attached to the camps could resist the Nazis by deliberately lowering the quality or speed of their work, or even by outright **sabotage**. Such resistance was extremely dangerous —the Nazis frequently punished workers when real accidents took place—but some forms of sabotage were hard to detect. A screw banged in with a hammer looked like one that had been screwed in with a screwdriver, but it was much more likely to give way when a product was used. Electrical connections could deliberately be left loose, just as seams on clothing could intentionally be made weak.

**These Jewish laborers at Janowska concentration camp in Ukraine worked the bone-crushing machine that was used to destroy evidence of mass murder. Many slave laborers tried to undermine the Nazi war effort by working slowly or inefficiently.**

**Rudolf Vrba's escape from Auschwitz helped alert the world to the fate overtaking the Hungarian Jews.**

# Escapes

Escape was another form of resistance. It was possible to escape from some camps, despite the presence of fences and guards, but staying free was another matter. People who escaped were usually in a weak condition before they started, and traveling across country was likely to weaken them further. To make matters worse, their shaved heads, striped clothing, and emaciated features made them easy to spot. Recaptured escapees were often executed in front of the other prisoners as an example.

Despite this, there were many escape attempts and a few that were successful. Two escapes from Auschwitz in the spring of 1944 —the first involving Slovak Jews Rudolf Vrba and Alfred Wetzler, the second involving Czech Jew Arnost Rosin and Polish Jew Czeslaw Mordowicz—probably saved tens of thousands of lives. Their reports (the "Auschwitz Protocols") about the ongoing massacre of Hungary's Jews persuaded U.S. president Franklin D. Roosevelt in July 1944 to threaten the bombing of the Hungarian capital of Budapest. His threat stopped the deportation of the final 170,000 Jews.

# Revolts

Given the high levels of supervision and security, it is incredible that any major revolts took place in the camps. Most camp revolts took place at the moment of maximum desperation, when the hopes of eventual survival had finally vanished. Faced with a choice between the smallest hope of victory through revolt and going meekly and certainly to their deaths, many chose to rise up. The overwhelming majority of resisters perished. Usually, a few were killed outright, a few escaped, and the vast majority were sent on to the gas chambers.

In Minsk Mazowiecki in central Poland in January 1943, 400 inmates of a labor camp barricaded themselves in a building rather than accept deportation to a death camp. The SS burned the building down. In August 1943, Jewish workers in Treblinka managed to set fire to several buildings; several guards were killed, and about 150 prisoners escaped. Half of them were hunted down and shot. Two months later, in the Sobibor death camp, Jewish girls who worked in the SS quarters managed to steal a few weapons and pass them on to the male prisoners. They attacked the SS and Ukrainian guards, killing more than 20. About 300 prisoners escaped to the forests nearby, and 30 of them survived the war.

The most important uprising inside Auschwitz was the *Sonderkommando* revolt of October 7, 1944. Although it resulted in several hundred deaths and few (if any) escapes, the uprising was not a complete failure. One of the four **crematoria** in Auschwitz was damaged beyond repair.

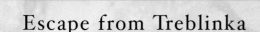

## Escape from Treblinka

Soon after the revolt in Treblinka in August 1943, the camp was closed, and the last prisoners were put to work destroying all traces of its existence. Knowing that they were likely to be killed when the job was finished, the prisoners kept an eager lookout for any chance of escape.

On September 2, 1943, thirteen of the prisoners were working outside the fence when one of them, an eighteen-year-old Polish Jew named Seweryn Klajnman, managed to kill their guard with a crowbar. He quickly put on the guard's uniform and marched the other twelve prisoners off down the road, cursing and screaming at them in typical SS style. One of the other prisoners knew the area well, and all thirteen managed to avoid being recaptured.

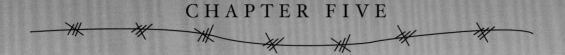

# CHAPTER FIVE

# Partisans

## Escape to the Forests

Most of the Polish and Soviet Jews who managed to evade the Nazis—by escaping from ghettos or camps or fleeing ahead of the advancing *Einsatzgruppen*—headed for the nearest forest. There was a simple reason that they chose this destination. In the large, flat expanse of the north European plain, these forests—some of which covered vast areas—offered the only real chance of safety.

The chance of survival, however, was small at best. Those Jews who reached the shelter of the trees were usually hungry, unarmed, and in poor health. The forests offered little in the way of food and significant hazards of their own, such as undrinkable water, vicious insects in the summer, and numbing cold in the winter. The forests were also likely to be occupied by bands of non-Jewish fugitives—Poles, Lithuanians, Russians, and Ukrainians—many of whom were every bit as **anti-Semitic**

## Tall and Proud

"We could hardly believe our eyes: armed Jewish men who I knew well from Novogrodek, who had escaped from the ghetto. They were no longer pale, frightened and downtrodden. They stood tall and proud. And, most important of all, they were armed with pistols, rifles, submachine guns and even machine guns."

*Resister Dov Cohen, describing his first meeting with the partisan Bielski Group in the Soviet Union after his escape from the Novogrodek Ghetto in 1943*

**This map shows the eastern European ghettos and forests.**

as the Nazis. Some local villagers and farmers were willing to help Jews, but others were more interested in what they could get from the Nazis for turning in escaped Jews. The Germans, meanwhile, had not forgotten the Jewish runaways and mounted frequent incursions into the forests, killing any Jews they came across. In such circumstances, the survival rate was bound to be low. Of the forty thousand Jews who fled to the forests in 1942, for example, fewer than one thousand lived to see the end of the war.

## Jewish Partisan Groups

Wherever possible, Jews banded together to form partisan groups, at first for self-defense and later for taking the fight back to the Nazis. Some never managed to establish themselves. In the forests to the north and east of Krakow, for example, escapees from the Krakow, Pinczow, and Radomysl Ghettos tried to set up partisan groups. Nazi drives to destroy them, however, proved almost completely successful.

**This group portrait shows the Bielski partisan group in the Nalibocka Forest. The photograph was taken between 1941 and 1944.**

Other Jewish partisan groups survived and prospered. Twenty-four-year-old Yehiel Grynszpan, the son of a local horse trader, reached the Parczew Forest in eastern Poland toward the end of 1942, where he quickly organized a partisan unit from the various Jewish runaways he came across. The group acquired weapons and food from local farmers and fought off the next German incursion into their territory. Two years later, when the Soviets took over the forest, Grynszpan's men were accepted as a special Jewish unit of the Soviet Partisan Army.

The Bielski Group, which operated in the Nalibocka Forest just west of Minsk in the Soviet Union, was much bigger than Grynszpan's force. The Bielskis were the only Jewish family in their village, and the three brothers—Tuvia, Asael, and Zus —set up their partisan group in March 1942. By the end of the year, the group boasted 150 members, and by mid-1943, despite punishing encounters with the Germans, it was looking after more than 1,200 Jewish women and children. At the group's camp deep in the forest, there was a bakery, cattle shed, leather works, metal workshop, hospital, and school.

A third group, the United Partisan Organization, led by poet and youth leader Abba Kovner, began life as a resistance group inside the Vilna Ghetto. The group decided to leave for the Rudninkai Forest only when it became clear that not enough of their fellow ghetto-dwellers were prepared to join a revolt.

## Fighting the Germans

The partisan groups devoted much of their efforts to protecting the large numbers of children and elderly in their care. All of the groups, however, mounted many actions against the German war machine and occupation authorities. They blew up trains, railroad tracks, and bridges, they attacked road convoys, and they pulled down telegraph poles. They also killed occupation officials and any local people found guilty of betraying Jews to the Nazi authorities.

Many of the partisan groups also made determined efforts to rescue as many as possible of the Jews still held in ghettos. Groups of partisans infiltrated the ghettos to smuggle people

## A World Turned Upside-Down

Jews who had grown up and worked in the cities found that they needed a very different set of skills to survive in the forests. Doctors and dentists were useful to the partisan groups, but people who had worked in business or other professions had little to offer. In order to survive in the forest, they needed help from those whom they had previously looked down upon—men like the Bielski brothers, who might not have known how to write but who knew how to build a fire in a frozen wilderness.

out, often at enormous risk. The Bielski partisans specialized in this activity, rescuing more Jews than any other Jewish group in occupied Europe.

Armed Jewish resistance was not, of course, confined to the forests of Poland and the western Soviet Union. In every country where Jews had been rounded up, some had slipped through the net, and many of them ended up in the local forests. Many Jews fought in the French and Belgian resistance movements, attacking German transportation and factories involved in war work. In April 1943, a Belgian group succeeded in derailing a train bound for Auschwitz and freeing many of the deportees.

# Deep Freeze

"The cold was unbearable. It was so cold that the birch trees were splitting from the low temperature. The crack of the trees splitting rang out like rifle shots in the forest. Some birds sitting in the trees froze to death and fell to the ground. It was impossible to sit through the night without a fire. We made small fires and sat around them. Our fronts were warm but our backs were so cold that the backs of our coats, wet from the falling snow, were frozen stiff as a board. Our faces were black from the smoke, and so were our hands, which we kept near the fire for warmth. Our clothes were full of holes from the sparks that jumped out of the fire, and the points of our boots were burned from keeping our feet so close to the flames.

"We could not stand in one place and had to move around to keep our feet from freezing. On very cold winter days, the early morning hours before sunrise were the coldest time of the day. The constant fear and the biting frost were terrible. Those of us who had a weapon felt a little more courageous."

*Harold Werner, who was sixteen years old when he joined*
*a partisan group in the forests of eastern Europe*

# The *Baumgruppe*

Jews also set up their own underground resistance groups in cities across occupied Europe. Although constantly threatened with discovery, these groups committed any acts of sabotage they could against the Nazis, knowing they would probably be killed. There was even a resistance group in Berlin, the heart of Nazi Germany. There, about seven hundred Jews worked at the Siemens Electrical Works, and a young communist named Herbert Baum persuaded some of them to join him in anti-Nazi activities. Incredibly, Baum's group (or the *Baumgruppe* in German) survived from 1937 to 1942, spending its nights distributing leaflets and painting slogans on walls under cover of darkness. The group also organized political training courses and underground cultural events. In May 1942, the *Baumgruppe* set fire to an anti-Jewish and anti-communist exhibition that was being held on the site where Nazi propaganda minister Joseph Goebbels had organized a famous book burning nine years earlier. This time, the activists were caught, and almost all of the *Baumgruppe* members were executed. Like other Jews who resisted the Nazis, they did so fully aware of what was likely to happen to them.

**Abba Kovner led the armed resistance in the Vilna Ghetto before its liquidation. He then commanded a partisan unit in the Rudninkai Forest.**

# CHAPTER SIX

# Not Enough Help

The Jewish resisters in the ghettos, camps, and forests needed all the help they could get. The possible sources of such help, inside and outside occupied Europe, included governments, churches, political parties and other social organizations, and individuals of all nationalities. Given that the greatest crime of modern times—and, quite possibly, the greatest crime in all history—was taking place, those Jewish resisters had reason to expect all the help that the rest of the world could offer. They did not get it.

## Governments and Churches in Occupied Europe

In occupied Europe, the governments of some German allies tried harder than others to save their Jewish populations. The Italian army protected Jews in Italian-occupied Yugoslavia and in territory annexed from France, while the Hungarian government of Admiral Miklos Horthy refused to deport Hungarian Jews until German troops invaded the country and forced them to do so. The Bulgarian government deported Jews from the parts of Greece and Yugoslavia that it had taken over, but refused to deport its own. When pressed by Germany, the king of Bulgaria ordered Jews held in camps to be freed, and farmers threatened to block the railroad tracks if the Germans attempted to take them north. After Finland deported eight Jews to Auschwitz, there was a public outcry. The Finnish government then refused, despite German pressure, to allow any further deportations and guaranteed the safety of the country's other two thousand Jews.

The governments of both Norway and Denmark cooperated with the Germans. While the pro-Nazi government in Norway was happy to deport Norwegian Jews, the Danish government was less eager to **collaborate**. Both governments, however, were frustrated by their own citizens. At least half of Norway's Jews were helped across the Swedish border by the Norwegian resistance. Almost all of Denmark's eight thousand Jews—a number including half-Jews as well as Christians who were married to Jews— were ferried across the sea to Sweden by fishermen and other boatowners. In contrast, the local authorities in France, Belgium, the Netherlands, Slovakia, Croatia, Romania, and Greece did little or nothing to protect their Jewish citizens from deportation and murder.

**NEDERLAND IN DEN OORLOG ZOOALS HET WERKELIJK WAS**

**ONZE VERNEDERING II**

De Jodenvervolging ingezet - Pogrom in de hoofdstad - Hun ontrechting en uitplundering - Westerbork - Het ghetto van Warschau - Theresienstadt - Vernichtungslager. Minister van Staat, beneden de maat - Ned. Oostcompagnie - Vernedering van de boeren - Moffen en Medici.

A. W. BRUNA & ZOON, UITGEVERSMAATSCHAPPIJ UTRECHT

**A Nazi poster from 1940 depicts the roundup of Jews in the occupied Netherlands.**

The leaders of European churches offered no notable help until the Holocaust was virtually complete. In Germany, both Protestant and Catholic churches took a stand in 1939–1941 against the Nazis' murdering of the mentally ill, but neither church spoke out against the persecution, deportation, and mass murder of the Jews. Throughout Europe, while many Christian churchgoers bravely spoke, acted, and organized on the Jews' behalf, the church leaders remained shamefully silent.

## Governments Outside Occupied Europe

The governments at war with Germany condemned the Nazis' treatment of the Jews but took no real steps to save them. At first, they even opposed Jewish emigration from Germany, Poland, and Romania, arguing that the Jews wanted to emigrate

## A Great Escape

Since the Nazis considered the Danes to be fellow Aryans, their occupation of Denmark was infinitely less harsh than their occupation of Poland or the western Soviet Union. The Nazis did, however, have every intention of deporting Denmark's Jews and half-Jews to Auschwitz. When this became known, both the Danish king and leading church authorities spoke out strongly against it, urging their fellow citizens to protect the Jews in their midst. Warned in advance that roundups for the deportation were to take place on the night of October 1, 1943, thousands of Danes of all ages and classes joined together to organize a great escape. The vast majority of the country's eight thousand Jews were delivered to a waiting fleet of small boats and carried across the sea to Sweden and safety.

**Danish Jews are ferried across the sea to Sweden in a fishing boat during the "Great Escape" of September 1943.**

only because they were being treated badly by their governments. The answer, officials said, was stopping persecution, not increasing emigration. This was only part of the story. None of the governments wanted to accept large numbers of Jewish **refugees**—partly because individuals in those governments were themselves anti-Semitic, and partly because they feared an anti-Semitic reaction from their own voters. When Romania offered to send 70,000 Jews to Palestine in February 1943, the British (who were in control of Palestine) refused. The U.S. State Department demonstrated even less sympathy, in some places obstructing the issuing of **visas** to Jewish refugees.

Once the war began, the Allies' demand for **unconditional surrender** ruled out any negotiations with the Nazis, even if those negotiations might have saved Jewish lives. The Allies also insisted on using all military resources just for military ends and said that rescue efforts would hamper the war. This insistence meant that no resources were diverted for operations that may have slowed the Holocaust, such as bombing the death camps or the railroads that fed them with victims.

## Peter Deman

Some Jews who escaped from Hitler's Europe ventured back into it. In 1938, Peter Deman escaped from Austria to France, where he joined the French army. Captured by the Germans in 1940, he was not identified as a Jew and ended up in a prisoner-of-war camp. He escaped from the camp, joined the French Foreign Legion as a way of getting out of occupied France, and then deserted. Reaching Britain, he joined the Allies' Special Operations Executive, which mounted undercover efforts in occupied Europe. A few months later, Deman was parachuted back into France as an agent, determined to continue his fight against the murderers of his people.

After the war, many people assumed that the Allies had not realized the extent of the crime taking place in eastern Europe. It now seems clear, however, that by the end of 1942, at the very latest, the governments in Washington, D.C., London, and Moscow knew that millions of Jews were being murdered. Yet the governments did almost nothing to interfere with the killing until mid-1944, when they actively began urging certain neutral nations—Sweden, Spain, and Portugal, in particular—to intervene on behalf of the Hungarian Jews.

## Jews Beyond Hitler's Reach

The Jews who, by luck or foresight, lived outside the Nazis' area of control were less inclined than their governments to

**Jewish officers of the 2nd Polish Corps—which fought with the British and Americans in Italy—celebrate Passover in 1945 in the Italian city of Como.**

just wait for victory. Many had seen Nazi anti-Semitism at work in prewar Germany, and when the rumors of **genocide** began seeping out of occupied Europe, they tended to believe them. Influential Jewish organizations, such as the World Jewish Congress, and individuals—for example, the British publisher Victor Gollancz—tried hard to persuade governments of the need for immediate action, but without success.

Some Jews contributed to the effort against the Nazis by working on crucial research in the development of new technology, such as radar and atomic energy. Many thousands fought in the Allied armies. The British army had a Jewish brigade, and 133 of the Jews who served in the Soviet **Red Army** won the highest award for bravery ("Hero of the Soviet Union") that their country had to offer. Several thousand Jews from Palestine volunteered to fight alongside the British in Crete, Africa, and Italy; 32 of them were parachuted behind German lines. There were also many Jews among the British, U.S., and Soviet forces who liberated the concentration and labor camps.

## The Bermuda Conference

By April 1943, public demands for some sort of action to save the Jews had become too widespread for the governments of the West to ignore, and a conference was arranged on the Atlantic island of Bermuda to defuse public protest. During the conference, which debated the refugee issue, delegates received frequent reports of the Warsaw Ghetto uprising, but they showed no sign of being moved by that struggle. On the contrary, they just kept repeating their usual argument, that rescue efforts were likely to get in the way of the war effort and should not be attempted. One American Jew who had pleaded for action observed, "If six million cattle had been slaughtered, there would have been more interest."

# CHAPTER SEVEN

# Gentiles Who Made a Difference

Oskar Schindler (left), with two of the Jews whom he helped to save, at a reunion in 1946. In 1962, he was named one of the Righteous Among the Nations by Yad Vashem, the Israeli government authority responsible for documenting and keeping alive the memory of the Holocaust.

## Dying for the Jews

Father Maximilian Kolbe, a Polish monk, was sent to the Auschwitz concentration camp early in the war. When the camp authorities decided that ten prisoners should be starved to death in retaliation for an escape attempt, Father Kolbe volunteered to take one of the condemned men's places. His offer was accepted. The man whose place he took survived the war. Through the years of the Holocaust, hundreds of gentiles like Father Kolbe sacrificed their own lives in the hope of saving others.

## Ordinary People

Although people of many nations actively participated in the Nazi genocide, particularly in eastern Europe, other people in those same nations risked their lives to help Jews. There was nothing obviously special about these people, yet they acted bravely and righteously. There was Leopold Socha, a Polish smuggler who came across twenty-one Jews escaping in the sewers of Lvov. He did his best to keep them fed and clothed until the Red Army arrived. There was Yanis Lipke, a Latvian farm worker who sheltered Jews from the Riga Ghetto, and Irene Gut Opdyke, a seventeen-year-old Polish girl who began by slipping food through a hole in the wall of the Radom Ghetto and ended by smuggling Jews into the nearby forest. Before the rise of the Nazis, Poland was considered a much more hostile environment for Jews than Germany, but thousands of non-Jewish Poles were shot for offering assistance to Jews.

## Churchmen

Although the churches in general did little to oppose the Nazis, some individual church officials showed considerably more courage. Jules-Gérard Saliège, the archbishop of Toulouse, was the first churchman publicly to criticize the deportation of Jews from France. Polish nuns belonging to the Congregation of

### Jan Pauvlavicius

Jan Pauvlavicius was a Lithuanian carpenter in the city of Kovno. He was already sheltering several Jews in his cellar when the Nazis, prior to abandoning the city, made preparations to kill the remaining inhabitants of the ghetto. Using his skills as a carpenter, Pauvlavicius constructed a hidden room in the cellar to accommodate an additional eleven Jews, and he managed to keep them all fed until the arrival of the Soviet Red Army.

**Raoul Wallenberg (above), a Swedish diplomat, saved the lives of thousands of Hungarian Jews. On the right is one of the lifesaving letters of protection he issued during his time in Budapest.**

Franciscan Sisters of the Family of Mary hid hundreds of Jewish children in their homes.

# Diplomats

Although governments on all sides said and did little to slow or stop the Holocaust, some of their representatives took crucial steps, acting on their own. Both Chiune Sugihara, Japanese **consul** in Kovno, and Aristides de Sousa Mendes, Portuguese consul-general in Bordeaux, ignored their orders and issued thousands of lifesaving visas to Jews fleeing the Nazis. Both men lost their jobs as a result.

Raoul Wallenberg, a Swedish diplomat, saved even more Jews than Sugihara or Sousa Mendes. Sent to Budapest in the summer of 1944 by the Swedish government, he quickly issued visas to more than six hundred Hungarian Jews. (Many

Hungarian Jews had already been deported, but hundreds of thousands remained.) When the Hungarian **fascists**—called the Arrow Cross—seized power in October 1944, Wallenberg rented 32 buildings where 15,000 more Jews could shelter under the Swedish flag. Authorized by his government to issue another 4,500 visas, he handed out three times that number. When the SS tried to march thousands of Jews out of Hungary, Wallenberg followed and handed out Swedish visas to Jews on the spot. He even had Jews removed from trains heading for Auschwitz and got them into shelters. As the Red Army neared the city and an SS general made plans to kill the remaining 70,000 Jews in the ghetto, Wallenberg threatened to see him hanged as a war criminal. The general abandoned his plans.

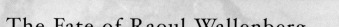

## The Fate of Raoul Wallenberg

When the Red Army finally arrived in Budapest on January 13, 1945, the threat of deportation and death was finally lifted from the Hungarian Jews who remained there. Those Jews, however, were living in terrible circumstances. On January 17, Raoul Wallenberg drove to Soviet headquarters at Debrecen to present a plan for feeding and housing the Jews in the weeks to come. He was never heard from again, and his fate remains uncertain to this day. It seems certain that he was imprisoned by the Soviet authorities, maybe on suspicion of being a U.S. spy. In 1955, the Soviet foreign minister announced that Wallenberg had died of a heart attack in 1947, but a recent investigation concluded that he was actually executed that year. Both reports conflict with rumors of sightings of Wallenberg in Soviet labor camps during the 1950s and 1960s. Whatever his actual fate, it was a tragic and bitterly unfair end for the courageous man who had saved so many lives in the six months preceding his disappearance.

# Germans

Most Germans were not willing to take a stand against their government's persecution and murder of the Jews. Some Germans refused to believe that things were as bad as others said, and many—after years of anti-Semitic propaganda—were quite willing to accept the deportation of the Jews to labor and concentration camps. Many Germans who knew about the mass killings decided that it had nothing to do with them. They were too busy fighting the war, they told themselves. Many believed, anyway, that they could not do anything about the situation.

A few did not feel so powerless. Oskar Schindler was a German businessman who came to Krakow in occupied Poland with the intention of making money. He set up a factory making kitchen equipment and staffed it with Jewish workers, who were inexpensive to employ. In 1942 and 1943, the Jews of the Krakow Ghetto were rounded up for deportation, and Schindler was an eyewitness to the cruelties of his fellow Germans. Eager to keep his Jewish workforce for business reasons, and eager to save them for compassionate reasons, he used all his skills and

## In the Town of Bialystok

The Polish town of Bialystok was notable for the number of Germans who actively helped the Jews. Two textile mill managers named Schade and Beneschek had contact with the local Jewish resistance organization, which they supplied with weapons, information, false documents, and money. The German in charge of one of the mill motor pools allowed Jews to use his car to transport weapons and people to the nearby forests; and several German soldiers stationed in the town donated radio sets and more weapons to the Jewish resistance. Other Germans smuggled arms into the ghetto and organized the escape of twenty Jews from the town's prison.

**SS guards watch over a departing column of Jews during the liquidation of the Krakow Ghetto in Poland in March 1943. This event was one reason Oskar Schindler decided to help the Jews whom he employed.**

influence to prevent them from ending up in the gas chambers. When the Nazis pulled out of Krakow, Schindler managed to get both his factory and workforce transferred to occupied Czechoslovakia. When the train carrying his female workers ended up in Auschwitz by accident, he forced the death camp's authorities to let them go. By the end of the war, Schindler had abandoned any idea of making profits—and had, in fact, bankrupted himself—but he had saved more than 1,500 Jews.

Schindler was not alone. Other German factory owners, such as Julius Madritsch, in Tarnow, and Otto Weidt, in Berlin, did all they could to save their Jewish employees.

## The Miracle of Resistance

The non-Jews who resisted the Nazis on the Jews' behalf each did so in ways that were appropriate to their position. They used whatever influence they had to save as many Jews as they could. All of them risked something, and many risked their lives. If it sometimes seems shameful that so many people did so little, it also seems a miracle that some people did so much.

# Time Line

**1933**  Nazi Party comes to power in Germany.

**1939**  September: German attack on Poland begins World War II; *Einsatzgruppen* units follow regular army units into Poland.
Fall: Nazis decide to kill all of Europe's Jews.

**1942**  March: Bielski brothers set up partisan group in Nalibocka Forest.
May: *Baumgruppe* destroys Nazi exhibition in Berlin.
July: Deportations from Warsaw Ghetto to Treblinka begin.
Anne Frank and her family go into hiding in Amsterdam.
Winter: Yehiel Grynszpan organizes Jewish partisan group in Parczew Forest.

**1943**  January: Resistance in Czestochowa is followed by massive Nazi retaliation;
revolt takes place in the Minsk Mazowiecki labor camp;
first serious armed resistance occurs in Warsaw Ghetto.
February: Romanian offer to send 70,000 Jews to Palestine is refused by Britain.
April: Bermuda Conference delegates reject idea of rescuing Jews from Europe.
April 19: Warsaw Ghetto uprising begins; ends in mid-May.

August: Revolt takes place in Treblinka death camp.
September 2: Seweryn Klajnman and twelve others escape from Treblinka.
October: Danish citizens help Denmark's Jewish population escape to Sweden; prisoners escape from the Sobibor death camp.

**1944**  Spring: Rudolf Vrba, Alfred Wetzler, Arnost Rosin, and Czeslaw Mordowicz escape from Auschwitz and provide the Allies with information on the massacre of Hungarian Jews.
June: Mala Zimetbaum and Edward Galinski escape from Auschwitz.
July: Threat of bombing Budapest, Hungary, by United States halts deportation of Hungarian Jews to Auschwitz.
Summer: Raoul Wallenberg begins issuing Swedish visas to Hungarian Jews.
August: Frank family is betrayed to the Nazis.
October: *Sonderkommando* revolt in Auschwitz; Hungarian fascist group Arrow Cross seize power in Hungary.

**1945**  January: Red Army arrives in Budapest; Wallenberg is taken away by Soviet authorities.

# Glossary

**allies:** people, groups, or nations that agree to support and defend each other. "The Allies" were the nations that fought together against Germany in World War I and World War II.

**anti-Semitic:** expressing prejudice against Jews.

**civilian:** person who is not serving in the armed forces.

**collaborate:** actively assist foreign occupiers of a country.

**communist:** person who believes in the principles of communism, a political system in which the government owns and runs the nation's economy. (A Communist with a capital "C" is a member of the Communist Party.)

**concentration camp:** prison camp set up by the Nazis to hold Jews and other victims of the Nazi regime. Many prisoners held in these camps were never tried or given a date of release.

**consul:** agent appointed by a government to represent its interests and citizens in a foreign nation.

**crematorium:** building in which bodies are burned. The plural is *crematoria*.

**death camp:** another term for extermination camp.

**deport:** forcibly remove from a place.

*Einsatzgruppen:* special SS units operating behind the advancing German army and ordered to murder Jews and other enemies of the Nazis.

**emigration:** leaving a country of residence to go and live somewhere else.

**extermination camp:** place set up by Nazis in which they murdered large numbers of people.

**fascist:** person who believes in the principles of fascism, a political system controlled by a dictator and under which no disagreement with authority is permitted.

**gas chamber:** airtight room or other space in which people are gassed to death.

**genocide:** deliberate murder or attempted murder of a whole people.

**gentile:** person who is not Jewish.

**ghetto:** usually poor and overcrowded part of a city, occupied by a minority group because of social, legal, or economic pressure.

**Gypsy:** member of a group that includes the Roma and Sinti peoples, who live mostly in Europe. Gypsies are traditionally nomadic, meaning they move from place to place.

**Hanukkah:** eight-day Jewish holiday, also called the Festival of Lights, celebrating the rededication of the Temple of Jerusalem after it had been defiled.

**homosexual:** person attracted to others of the same sex.

**identity papers:** official documents carried to prove who a person is.

***Judenrat*:** council of Jews set up by the Nazis to govern a ghetto. The plural is *Judenräte*.

***Kapo*:** prisoner placed in charge of work teams in prison camps.

**labor camp:** camp in which prisoners are forced to perform hard labor.

**Middle Ages:** period of European history from about A.D. 500 to 1500.

**noncooperation:** form of protest involving the refusal to cooperate rather than outright resistance.

**partisan:** fighter who lives and fights behind enemy lines or within occupied territory.

**Red Army:** army of the Soviet Union, the nation that was one of the Allies by the end of World War II.

**refugee:** person who flees or is forced to leave his or her own home or country and who seeks refuge elsewhere.

**resistance:** opposition to or the fight against an overpowering force.

**revolt:** rebellion against authority.

**sabotage:** deliberate damage done to undermine enemy activities.

***Sonderkommando*:** Jewish prisoner in death camps who dealt with the bodies of those who were murdered.

**SS:** short for *Schutzstaffel*, a Nazi elite force also known as "the blackshirts."

**terrorist:** person who performs acts of violence in order to make a political point or force a change in government policy.

**Third Reich:** name given by the Nazis to their regime. The name means "third empire," following the First Reich (the medieval Holy Roman Empire) and the Second Reich (1870–1918).

**unconditional surrender:** complete surrender without any conditions.

**visa:** official document allowing a person to enter a country.

# Further Resources

## Books

Axelrod, Toby. *Rescuers Defying the Nazis: Non-Jewish Teens Who Rescued Jews* (Teen Witnesses to the Holocaust). Rosen Publishing Group, 1999.

Frank, Anne. *The Diary of a Young Girl.* Doubleday, 1995.

Glick, Susan. *Heroes of the Holocaust* (History Makers). Lucent Books, 2003.

Sherrow, Victoria. *The Righteous Gentiles* (Holocaust Library). Lucent Books, 1998.

Shuter, Jane. *Resistance to the Nazis* (The Holocaust). Heinemann Educational Books, 2002.

## Web Sites

**The Holocaust: Crimes, Heroes and Villains**
www.auschwitz.dk
Web site about those involved in the Holocaust, with biographies, poetry, photos, and more.

**The Holocaust History Project**
www.holocaust-history.org
Archive of documents, photos, and essays on various aspects of the Holocaust.

**Holocaust Survivors**
www.holocaustsurvivors.org
Interviews, photos, and sound recordings of survivors of the Holocaust.

**The Museum of Tolerance's Multimedia Learning Site**
motlc.wiesenthal.org
Educational Web site of the Simon Wiesenthal Center, a Jewish human rights agency.

**Non-Jewish Holocaust Victims**
www.holocaustforgotten.com
A site dedicated to the Nazis' five million non-Jewish victims.

**United States Holocaust Memorial Museum**
www.ushmm.org
Personal histories, photo archives, and museum exhibits of the Holocaust.

## About the Author

David Downing has been writing books for adults and children about political, military, and cultural history for thirty years. He lives in Britain.

# Index